MANAGING ACROSS CULTURES

A Learning Framework

Managing Across Cultures
A Learning Framework

Meena S. Wilson
Michael H. Hoppe
Leonard R. Sayles

Center for Creative Leadership
Greensboro, North Carolina

The Center for Creative Leadership is an international, nonprofit educational institution founded in 1970 to advance the understanding, practice, and development of leadership for the benefit of society worldwide. As a part of this mission, it publishes books and reports that aim to contribute to a general process of inquiry and understanding in which ideas related to leadership are raised, exchanged, and evaluated. The ideas presented in its publications are those of the author or authors.

The Center thanks you for supporting its work through the purchase of this volume. If you have comments, suggestions, or questions about any Center publication, please contact John R. Alexander, President, at the address given below.

Center for Creative Leadership
Post Office Box 26300
Greensboro, North Carolina 27438-6300

©1996 Center for Creative Leadership
Reprinted 2002

CCL No. 173

Library of Congress Cataloging-in-Publication Data

Wilson, Meena S.
    Managing across cultures : a learning framework / Meena S. Wilson, Michael H. Hoppe, Leonard R. Sayles
      p.   cm.
    Includes bibliographical references.
    ISBN 1-882197-25-9
    1. International business enterprises—Management. 2. Management—Cross-cultural studies. 3. Comparative management. 4. Intercultural communication. I. Hoppe, Michael H. II. Sayles, Leonard R. III. Title.
HD62.4.W59 1996
658—dc20
                                                                96-36687
                                                                     CIP

For My Parents,
Atam Dev and Vimla Nagrath Surie

Meena S. Wilson

Table of Contents

Preface

In developing the learning framework presented in this paper, we have consulted current research in the fields of anthropology, cross-cultural psychology, and international business management (see the Appendix) and have attempted to integrate the concepts we found there into a tool that managers and employees can use to understand the behavior of people from a variety of cultural backgrounds.

We want to emphasize that our framework, which currently has seven dimensions, is a provisional one. These dimensions will be empirically tested for reliability and validity when we administer a survey (the *Intercultural Values Questionnaire,* or IVQ) to an international sample of managers and executives. (The scales of the IVQ are the same as the dimensions of the framework.) Ultimately we hope to link cultural values to three domains of managerial behavior: (1) relating to others, (2) accomplishing work, and (3) responding to change. The results from the IVQ survey will thus help us refine the learning framework presented in this paper.

Acknowledgments

This publication would not have been possible without the help of many people. We would like to thank Nancy Adler, John Fulkerson, Philip Hamer, and Mark Petersen for their careful review of the final draft. We have followed several of their suggestions for framing difficult concepts and avoiding cultural bias.

We are also indebted to our internal reviewers—Lily Kelly-Radford, Jean Leslie, Gordon Patterson, Marian Ruderman, Walter Tornow, and Ellen Van Velsor—who helped us discover how to make these concepts more accessible to practicing managers.

In addition, Marcia Horowitz is to be thanked for her sound editorial advice on organizing the content, as are Debbie Nelson and Lee Stine for their assistance with typing different versions of this report.

Among those who were unfailing in their personal support and encouragement of the lead author, gratitude is due Robert Burnside, Maxine Dalton, Cindy McCauley, and Martin Wilcox.

This publication has also benefited from fieldwork conducted at Kraft General Foods, Inc.; Merck & Co.; and Philip Morris International. These companies provided financial support for the research and made their expatriate managers available for interviews.

Introduction

Recently the U.S. manager of a water resources project in Indonesia ran into trouble when he made what he thought was a routine administrative move to restrict access to the office copy machine. The memo communicating the decision to deny other offices in the vicinity use of the machine was declared "insensitive to Indonesian ways" (Scott-Stevens, 1991) and was widely regarded as unfriendly, unilateral, and even unethical. Eventually, after a series of similar incidents, the manager was dismissed.

As the above incident highlights, managing in a multicultural setting can be very challenging. Culture strongly influences how one behaves and how one understands the behavior of others, and cultures vary in the behaviors they find proper and acceptable.

But it is not only the expatriate manager who faces this kind of challenge. If you are a member of a multinational project team, if you have a domestic assignment that involves people who have emigrated from other countries or colleagues from a minority culture in the U.S., or if you must communicate with business associates who live in other parts of the world, you must deal with similar cultural issues.

How can such challenges be met? Cultural synopses of individual countries, with their lists of *do*s and *don't*s, provide some insight, but their usefulness is limited by the complexity of culture, as well as by current managerial conditions: You often have to deal with people from several different cultures at once, and, because opportunities develop quickly and must be pursued without delay, you may have to go into a meeting, either face-to-face or at a distance, with little or no time to prepare for a particular culture.

Also, such synopses cannot help you with the part that your own culture plays in any interaction. This important element is easily overlooked because your own culture is so much a part of you that you are unaware of its influence. You are, as social scientists say, embedded in it.

In this paper we present a framework that will help you learn from your cross-cultural experiences: by making you aware of the beliefs and values that underlie the workplace preferences of managers in the U.S. and, con-comitantly, by providing you with a way to understand the value preferences of people from other cultures. Thus, you will be able to learn as you go, whatever managerial conditions you encounter.[†]

[†] This paper focuses on managerial thinking. In an upcoming paper we will explore the behaviors that managers need to adopt to gather information about cultural norms different from their own.

This framework was developed by integrating previous research in the fields of anthropology, cross-cultural psychology, and international business management (Hall, 1981; Hoppe, 1990; Laurent, 1983; Ronen, 1986; Sayles, 1995; Schwartz, 1993; Triandis, McCusker, & Hui, 1990; see also the Appendix). We are particularly indebted to Geert Hofstede (1980) and to Charles Hampden-Turner and Fons Trompenaars (1993) for their research and insights.

Before presenting the framework, however, we should define some basic terms and processes, beginning with culture.

Culture can be broadly defined as a people's way of life. It develops over time and is shaped by the geography and history of a region. It is often narrowly associated with an individual's knowledge of formal social etiquette and of artistic, musical, and literary traditions, but culture encompasses all the institutions of a society—political, legal, economic, religious, educational, and so on.

Culture is both tangible and intangible, explicit and implicit (Hofstede, 1980; Schein, 1985; Trompenaars, 1993). At the tangible level, cultures are expressed by language, dress, food, social rituals, customs, holiday traditions, folk heroes, symbols, and artifacts. At the intangible level, cultures are built on beliefs and values. Usually, those who have been reared and remain in one culture are unconscious of their cultural beliefs and values.

Culture is clearly a complex phenomenon. One way of understanding it is through the following analogy: Culture is to a group what personality is to an individual. Just as an individual acquires a workable personality over his or her life, a human group develops a complex system of values and behaviors that aids the group's survival in an ever-evolving environment. Such a system of thinking, feeling, and acting has been described as a "collective programming of the mind which distinguishes the members of one group or category of people from another" (Hofstede, 1991, p. 5).

The idea central to this and over 150 other definitions of culture (Kroeber & Kluckhohn, 1952) is that there is a unifying pattern of beliefs and values that creates an identity for a group and for the individuals who are members of that group. These "unifying patterns" are akin to a "software of the mind" (Hofstede, 1991) with respect to beliefs about human nature; the relationship of humans to each other; the relationship of humans to the natural world; and concepts of activity, space, and time (Kluckhohn & Strodtbeck, 1961).

Beliefs and values are closely linked. Values are central beliefs about how one ought or ought not to behave, as well as about some end-state of existence that is worth or not worth attaining (Rokeach, 1973). Values, in this sense, come from a shared agreement among a majority of people within a culture that a general set of principles, standards, and qualities are important or desirable. Values are founded on ideals and create preferences for certain states of affairs over others.

Given these meanings of *culture* and *value,* for this report we propose the following definition:

> Culture is a pattern of shared values reflected in the preferences of groups of people for certain behaviors, attitudes, and systemic practices in their ideal work situation.

Underlying the pattern of shared values held by any single group of people are a number of fundamental dilemmas faced by everyone, regardless of culture (Hampden-Turner & Trompenaars, 1993). For example, there is the dilemma of authority: How should people with different levels of power and status behave toward each other—as equals or unequals?

Each culture can be understood as having a value that favors particular behaviors in situations that involve this dilemma.

Let's consider, for instance, a situation where the boss and a subordinate are working together and the boss wants a cup of coffee (or tea). Even an upper-echelon manager in certain Latin American cultures will attend to the personal needs of a superior by getting that person a cup of coffee when necessary. Only in the U.S. and some northern European countries is it likely that the boss who wants coffee will have to get it for him- or herself.

In our view, these behaviors are influenced by the dilemma of authority: Either humans are unequal, and those with higher status expect those with lower status to perform various tasks as needed, or humans are equal, and those with higher status do not expect those with lower status to perform tasks that are not directly work-related.

In this situation, as in most that people encounter, there is, of course, a choice—the subordinate can either bring or not bring the cup of coffee. Each culture has a value favoring a certain behavior in an authority situation, and it is very likely that people will select the course of action preferred by their culture.

It is important to note that the culture-behavior link is by no means simple. For instance, membership in a subculture on the basis of regionality, ethnicity, gender, age, religion, level of education, or socioeconomic class can significantly influence values and behavior; organizational culture, as determined by factors such as industry size, history, location, and integration of technology, can shape how country culture values are acted out; and individual personality can influence thoughts, feelings, and actions to a greater extent than cultural values.

It is also important to note that cultural values, which essentially comprise a hierarchy of ideals to which people refer in public settings, may not always translate into actual behavior. Individuals and groups do not invariably follow the guidelines of their culture. Values are expressions of preference and not absolute predictors of behavior.

Our understanding of the specific ways that culture influences behavior in business situations is reflected in the learning framework presented below. Each of its dimensions represents one of what we consider seven fundamental dilemmas that people of all cultures face at work (see Table 1).

Table 1
Learning Framework for Managers Working Across Cultures

1. **Source of Identity: Individual-Collective**
   To what degree should people pursue their own individual activities, achievements, and educational and business successes rather than contribute to the activities, achievements, and successes of their extended family, clan or ethnic group, or even company or division?

2. **Goals and Means of Achievement: Tough-Tender**
   How is success defined? Do the people in the culture strive for the tangible rewards of a high income and material satisfactions or the intangible rewards of good working relationships, time with family and friends, and satisfaction from spiritual development and volunteer work?

3. **Orientation to Authority: Equal-Unequal**
   How should people with different levels of authority, status, and power behave toward each other—as equals or unequals?

4. **Response to Ambiguity: Dynamic-Stable**
   How acceptable is uncertainty? Is loose or tight structure preferred for running the business organization?

5. **Means of Knowledge Acquisition: Active-Reflective**
   Which is valued more as a means of acquiring information and knowledge—action or reflection?

6. **Perspective on Time: Scarce-Plentiful**
   Is the orientation to the use of time urgent or relaxed?

7. **Outlook on Life: Doing-Being**
   Is mastery over nature or harmony with nature preferred? Is life experienced as an outcome of human effort or the workings of destiny or divine will?

We begin each section with a set of questions that describe the dilemma.

We believe that the possible responses to each dilemma can be understood as a continuum of choices, with clearly contrasted options at the two poles of the continuum. For any culture, it is possible to envision a process in which behaviors favoring one pole are reinforced to a greater degree than behaviors favoring the opposite pole. So each culture can be seen as exhibiting a pattern of preferences about the most desirable ways of thinking and acting. Thus, we next discuss each pole of the continuum, pointing out the preferences of U.S. managers.

Finally, we will discuss how the values tend to play out in the workplace.

Throughout, examples will be used to illustrate how values can affect workplace practices and behaviors. The following points should be kept in mind when reading these examples.

First, they are not meant to stereotype cultures or people—to say that this is the way that a person from a particular culture will invariably act. Rather they are meant to highlight the opposing orientations that people may have. They should be used as a means of understanding the values that underlie behavior. (We will say more about stereotyping in the section titled "Using the Framework.")

Second, because the motivations that drive a particular behavior may be complex, the examples we use to illustrate a particular value may actually demonstrate a combination of values. If a manager refuses a promotion, this could be understood as being influenced by a value relating to the dimension "Source of Identity" (oriented toward the Collective pole), the dimension "Goals and Means of Achievement" (oriented toward the Tender pole), or the dimension "Outlook on Life" (oriented toward the Being pole). A simple behavior may be influenced by any one or by a number of different values. In the continuing research related to our framework, we will investigate how combinations of values may affect attitudes (toward co-workers, bosses, the organization, work itself, and so on) and practices (in areas such as decision making, planning, work execution, and so on).

Finally, the examples presented here may seem to favor one value orientation over another. For instance, to some readers it may appear as if we consider the U.S. approach to be the best; others may think we see the U.S. way of doing things as causing problems. We are not making such judgments here. But the cultures in which we are embedded may affect how we have made our presentation, just as the cultures in which you are embedded will affect your understanding of this presentation.

Source of Identity: Individual-Collective

To what degree should people pursue their own individual activities, achievements, and educational and business successes rather than contribute to the activities, achievements, and successes of their extended family, clan or ethnic group, or even company or division?

At the Individual Pole

In societies near the Individual pole, people primarily look after their own interests and those of their immediate family. They expect, and are expected, to be self-reliant, show initiative, and chart their own careers.

Many people from the U.S. culture believe in the dignity and worth of each individual and see self-development and self-realization as worthy goals. U.S. movies frequently portray the lone hero who ignores all the rules of his community or society and yet is successful and admired. Rugged individualism is idealized in books, films, and on television.

Another illustration: Most English-language desk dictionaries include over one hundred words with *self-* as a prefix—for example, *self-confidence, self-control,* and *self-expression.* In most other languages, equivalent words, emphasizing the importance of the individual, do not exist.

At the Collective Pole

In societies near the Collective pole, people look after the interests of their extended family and clan or ethnic group. They expect, and are expected, to show loyalty to and support for their group in return for protection, a sense of belonging, and lifetime employment.

For example, in the cultures of Pakistan, Venezuela, and the island of Fiji in the South Pacific, interdependent behavior is much more usual. The following example is from Fiji:

> No man dreams of making a garden, or building a house, for the simple reason that he does not feel himself to have any individual existence. He is only one of a brotherhood or family and can only think and act with its other members. . . . If a garden is to be made, or a house to be built, the whole village assembles and the work is done. But for a man to attempt doing anything of the sort for himself is from a Fijian point of view either ridiculous or insolent. (Edwards, 1992, p. 81)

In the Workplace

These cultural values affect many practices and behaviors, of which we note the following.

Individual accountability. A central principle of Western management is to delegate as much decision-making authority and responsibility to the individual as competence and motivation merit. Associated with individual accountability is the tendency for managers to assume credit for jobs well done and look for the individuals who should be blamed when objectives are not achieved.

By contrast, in industrialized Japan, group accountability, through the "ringii" process, is the norm. In a Japanese company, enormous amounts of time may go toward accommodating the feelings of all those who will be affected by a decision, by consulting them through informal contacts, formal meetings, and correspondence. This practice of achieving consensus before a major commitment is announced leads to decision making that is time-consuming but decision implementation that is quick.

Career progress. In many modern organizations, career progress is based on the individual's ability to fulfill job responsibilities effectively. Effectiveness is rewarded by promotions. Promotions are desirable, lead to an increase in the scope of the manager's responsibilities, and may involve transfers to other departments and relocation.

The human resources manager of a global pharmaceutical company who had been assigned to the Far East discovered, to his surprise, that his greatest challenge was to persuade the company's Chinese, Malaysian, Taiwanese, and Korean managers to accept promotions. These managers did not wish to compete with their peers for career rewards or personal gain—nor were they interested in breaking their ties to their communities in order to assume cross-national responsibilities.

Private offices and privacy. The need for privacy in some cultures, especially in the West, is incomprehensible to people from several other cultures. In the U.S., privacy is seen as satisfying, and private offices help employees to get work done as individuals. Elsewhere, privacy is regarded as undesirable because it separates the individual from the group and seems lonely. Employees expect that work will be done by groups and do not like the isolation of individual offices.

Imagine the frustration on both sides when a worker from a culture that is near the Collective pole politely converses with a co-worker from a culture that is near the Individual pole. When the latter literally shows his colleague the door, each may be puzzled and upset by the other's behavior.

Candor. U.S. managers working in Latin American and other countries report that it is difficult to get subordinates to provide information about poor performance or about unfavorable situations or events. In many cultures people prefer not to deliver negative evaluations. "Saving face" is important; because social harmony is valued and sensitivity to others' feelings is the norm, instead of being straightforward, people try to be nonconfrontational and indirect.

Because managers and employees give agreeable responses even when they disagree with the views being expressed, listeners have to learn to detect negative reactions from very subtle cues. The Japanese, for example, are noted for expressing disapproval by a mild intake of breath, which makes only a low hissing sound.

Under such circumstances the open and direct approach favored by U.S. managers can be considered shockingly tactless or, worse, humiliating. Failures at work—mistakes, missed quotas or customers, or a botched order —can bring shame, not only to an employee's family but also to their ethnic group; so direct criticism of subordinates can be a crushing blow to them.

Loyalty to the company. In several Latin American, European, and Far Eastern cultures, employees take pride in being a part of a family and tend to think of their organization as surrogate family. In turn, their company adopts paternalistic employment practices such as long-term employment, preferential hiring of other family members, subsidized housing, and so on.

Belonging to the Toyota or Matsushita "family," for example, was a critical part of the personal identity of a Japanese worker, not unlike the feelings of U.S. employees who worked for IBM or Eastman Kodak in an earlier time. Thinking of the company as "extended family" in this way made these Japanese employees, at least in the past, willing to sacrifice personal time or vacations in favor of long working hours. Failing to meet one's moral obligation to work hard would bring shame to one's family. The government even considered requiring employees to take allotted vacation time (Sayles, research notes).

By contrast, in the U.S. and other countries near the Individual pole— such as the United Kingdom, Canada, and Ireland—the "new psychological employment contract" (Noer, 1993) is a more acceptable concept. Employees are encouraged to make a commitment not to their company but to their own careers and the type of work they do. Rather than loyally tying their fortune in life to an organization, individuals are advised to use the organization to improve their general competence and employability.

Loyalty to one's family and clan. In many parts of the world, particularly in the Middle and Far East, southern and eastern Europe, and

Latin America, both government and business executives in key positions expect payments for their approvals. These payments, known as *baksheesh* in several cultures, are customary practice and are regarded as part of their salary—they may be supporting over a dozen people in their extended family. The officials and executives would be disloyal if they did *not* use their position to increase family earnings or give preference in employment to family members such as their children and even cousins, uncles, nephews, and godchildren.

U.S. managers tend to see these payoffs as a demand for a bribe and regard this as a form of corruption. They can find themselves caught in a conflict between company rules forbidding payments and the difficulty, if not the impossibility, of carrying out business without payoffs.

U.S. managers also are likely to assume that most employees will not use their jobs as a means of favoring family and friends. The dilemma for the U.S. manager comes from a culturally shaped commitment to treating all people equally and fairly. Nepotism and favoritism based on family or ethnic affiliation are usually considered wrong. U.S. managers ideally want to apply the same standards and rules to everybody. Even when the ideal is not realized perfectly (as in the case of people of color), they have adopted the legal and organizational norm that favoritism is discriminatory and inequitable.

Goals and Means of Achievement: Tough-Tender

How is success defined? Do the people in the culture strive for the tangible rewards of a high income and material satisfactions or the intangible rewards of good working relationships, time with family and friends, and satisfaction from spiritual development and volunteer work?

At the Tough Pole

In societies near the Tough pole, people value—both in themselves and in others—ambition, competitiveness, and decisiveness. Big, for them, is beautiful. Work, or their "job," plays a central role in their life. They wish to excel, greatly admire achievers, and covet the results of achievement.

Among the many "implicit cultural assumptions" of people in the U.S. cited by L. Robert Kohls (1981, p. 14) are the following: competition and free enterprise, an action orientation, materialism, and a problem-solving orientation.

At the Tender Pole

In cultures near the Tender pole, people strive for cooperation and harmony within the group. Mutual obligation is emphasized, as is the sharing of material and nonmaterial resources. Small is beautiful. They prefer the slogan "Work to live" rather than "Live to work." They feel sympathy for those who are less fortunate.

In cultures such as those of the Netherlands and Indonesia, if there is a conflict between work and social relationships, social relationships are likely to take priority. Though this may seem like a weakness of character, in these cultures a great deal of time is devoted to friendships. Frequent and unexpected visits between friends are the norm, favors and gifts are freely exchanged, and both criticism and caretaking behaviors are more common between those with affective ties. Such ties also involve a certain amount of dependency and obligation.

In the Workplace

These values affect the following practices and behaviors.

Competition and cooperation. The U.S. culture encourages competition so that continually higher standards of achievement are set and met. Competitive challenge is seen as making each person perform at his or her highest level of capability. Because the job must be done and tangible achievements are valued, individuals who give top priority to the bottom line and get results are the ones considered most effective and are usually well rewarded for their efforts. Individuals come to believe that their success in life comes from besting others. The Darwinian concept of the survival of the fittest is often referenced.

The economic system of free enterprise is the institutional expression of this value. It is based on the strong belief that a highly competitive economy will create the most rapid technological and social progress.

The value placed on competitive individual achievement is so great in the U.S. that incentives rewarding team productivity are sometimes viewed with disfavor. When working abroad, some U.S. managers come to see, for the first time, how dominating and assertive U.S. managers can be, compared to their counterparts, and how much easier it is for some non-U.S. managers to work in teams.

However, they may also observe the downside of norms favoring overly cooperative attitudes. When competition is alien to their culture and values, employees are reluctant to assert themselves and may suppress their ideas. They also tend not to respond, at least at the outset, to competition-based incentives.

Modesty. The value placed on social harmony is an inducement to be modest as well. Managers in many parts of the world—for example, Finland, South Korea, Thailand, Costa Rica, and Guatemala—rarely refer to individual accomplishments or openly talk about personal successes. They believe that one person is seldom responsible for the great achievements that come about in an organization. Similarly, it is common for people from these cultures to deny their expertise or talents and to refer to the effectiveness of others in glowing terms. In such cultures U.S. managers often seem offensively boastful.

The ease with which U.S. organizations utilize, and individuals seek and accept, feedback and help toward self-development can be perceived as immodest and narcissistic by people from other cultures. Edward Hall (personal conversation, SIETAR Conference, 1994) recounts how amusing Native Americans found him to be when, starting his first job among them as a 26-year-old, he continually asked, "How am I doing?" His excessive preoccupation with gaining recognition for his efforts and performance seemed unbalanced to them.

Separating family considerations from work life. Historically, not letting family and personal life interfere with achieving career objectives has been important in large U.S. organizations. The U.S. is somewhat unusual in presuming that family and work priorities should be clearly separated. Until recently, for example, companies freely disregarded the family cost of frequent moves. Family considerations, such as the effect of disrupting the schooling of children or the need to take care of elderly and ailing parents, still tend to be ignored when expatriate assignments are made.

In the U.S. there is now increasing concern for family issues in the workplace; however, the repercussions of work intruding on family life are usually more serious abroad. A U.S. expatriate manager proudly reported an atypical decision that he had made: He refused his boss's direct order (via a fax from the U.S.) to cancel all vacations for the upcoming two weeks because of an internal crisis in the company. The expatriate manager acted instead on his knowledge that his European subordinates would not take kindly to a sacrifice of family commitments (Sayles, research notes).

Thus, in many countries the role of the employee as a family member is more clearly recognized and respected. A manager found a notable contrast in the tone of the professional recommendations given him by former supervisors from the U.S. and the Netherlands. The U.S. supervisor focused solely on the manager's professional achievements; the Dutch supervisor also commended him as "a loyal friend who takes care of his family" (Sayles, research notes).

Orientation to Authority: Equal-Unequal

How should people with different levels of power and status behave toward each other—as equals or unequals?

At the Equal Pole

In societies near the Equal pole, people have come to expect that differences in power among them will be minimized. Those with and without power see themselves as having equal value as human beings. Hierarchical structures are seen as merely an expression of role inequality, not personal inequality, and are accepted as convenient and efficient. Subordinates want their superiors to consult with them and be accessible. Privileges based on status are downplayed.

The U.S. is a young country, populated primarily by immigrants. Compared to other cultures, there has been a lack of emphasis on ancestry and family origins. People in the U.S. are mobile as well. All of this has discouraged the growth of aristocratic privileges and class distinctions.

Equality is one of the values most cherished by people in the U.S. They like to think that anyone, regardless of gender, race, or other background factors, has the same chance of succeeding.

The view that rank and privilege should be attained by work and not by birth is a U.S. tradition that dates back to the early immigrants and pioneers. The hardships that they faced dignified labor because all had to participate equally in establishing new settlements; no one could insist that he or she be served by another. Thus, people in the U.S. believe that status must be achieved and not inherited.

These beliefs often foster an easy informality between people, even between employees from the highest and lowest levels in an organization. The use of first names is typical, emphasizing that all humans have been created equal.

At the Unequal Pole

In societies near the Unequal pole, people expect and accept large differences in power, status, and privileges. They view inequality among them as existential in nature. Hierarchies, such as class systems, are considered an expression of this inequality, and hierarchical systems are seen as satisfying needs for structure, security, and dependence. Subordinates prefer their superior to take the initiative, make the decisions, and take care of their needs. Those with status are granted privileges, not only in work settings but in all arenas of their life.

Cultures such as those of France, Greece, and Mexico give rise to organizations in which top management has almost life-and-death power over subordinates. Absolute obedience is demanded, in return for which employees are likely to receive protection from a variety of adversities, as long as they demonstrate consistent loyalty to their boss—*patron* or *godfather* in Latin America and Italy, respectively.

Latin-born managers who begin working in the United States find it hard to understand why their subordinates resent their insistence on unchallenged authority and substantial deference. In their view this great power is only their due, and they exercise it in benign ways that protect and care for their dependent charges. Why, they wonder, should this system of care and responsibility be resented?

Of course, in countries where the exercise of power is unchecked, people with status—for example, government leaders—may feel entitled to use their positions to accrue incredible personal wealth. This may appall the U.S. manager.

At the same time, U.S. managers expatriated to countries where people habitually defer to their leaders may come to enjoy the variety of privileges that are automatically granted to them. They see how their wishes become commands, and the experience of being highly influential can be addictive.

In the Workplace

These values affect the following practices and behaviors.

Hiring and promotion based on "achieved" versus "ascribed" status. The core of the U.S. ideal is that people should be given recognition because of what they have achieved, not because of ethnicity, religion, class, accent, level of education, or where they attended college or preparatory school. This difference in beliefs about how status should be gained is described by scholars as valuing "status by achievement" more than "status by ascription."

Given this value, U.S. managers become distressed when they observe in many countries that having gone to the right school (for example, one of les Grandes Écoles in France), belonging to the right family and being part of an elite class, or having the right accent can be as important in hiring and promotion decisions as on-the-job performance and technical qualifications.

Deference. In developing countries it is not unusual to find managers who seem totally absorbed with status symbols. They monitor their own and others' behaviors toward people who have greater or lesser status. Although U.S. managers can be cavalier about such matters, in most other parts of the world anxiety connected with giving and getting proper respect is a consequential issue. Managers from some other countries go to great lengths to avoid unintentionally insulting peers or superiors by failing to show proper respect.

Some ways of showing respect to a particular person are: arranging to spend time frequently conversing with that person, even though you may see no need for such a contact; adjusting seating at meetings so that the person sits close to those of high status; personally accompanying the person to his or her hotel, home, or transportation; and directing attention to the person by mentioning his or her name and accomplishments.

The norm in U.S. organizations may not be as close to the Equal pole on this dimension as many would like to believe, given the egalitarian attitudes of people in the U.S. in general. Some European managers, for example, seem to show little respect for authority based on titles or positions in a hierarchy. In a six-hour business simulation that included four tiers of management, managers from some European cultures were more likely to ignore the president or challenge him at meetings (Wall & McHenry, 1989).

Lack of delegation. High-level leaders in traditional cultures expect that almost every decision will be referred to them before being made final. Organizations in such cultures offer little empowerment at the lower levels. It is not considered good leadership to provide information about goals and values to enable subordinates to make choices. Thus, subordinates have few guides or cues as to what decisions would likely be acceptable to their superiors. In fact, even technical decisions in such cultures are likely to be made on the basis of the intuition or the gut feeling of a top executive, in contrast to relying on technical experts and specialists.

Under these circumstances, a mystique surrounds the leader, and the allegiance of subordinates is to the leader personally, not to the organization. The charismatic power of the leader makes it difficult to delegate authority to other managers. Needless to say, it does not make sense to negotiate with anyone but the head person.

Some years ago IBM lost the opportunity to negotiate a valuable computer contract when it sent a highly successful, intelligent, but very young sales representative to meet with a senior executive in a Mexican firm. When the Mexican executive observed that the negotiator from IBM was many years his junior and had an unimpressive job title, he was insulted and terminated their meeting after peremptory introductions (Sayles, research notes).

Response to Ambiguity: Dynamic-Stable

How acceptable is uncertainty? Is loose or tight structure preferred for running the business organization?

At the Dynamic Pole

In societies near the Dynamic pole, people accept ambiguity as a natural part of life. They do not shy away from conflict, dissent, or competition. In fact, they view these as potentially beneficial. They value flexibility, adaptability, and change and are open to adjusting existing rules or regulations as the situation demands. They are willing to take risks even in unfamiliar circumstances.

A can-do mentality is pervasive in the U.S. The words *new* and *improved* exemplify the value placed on development and innovation. Traditional practices are often ignored or satirized, and the status quo is usually questioned. These attitudes provide the drive, excitement, and energy that can be a source of organizational effectiveness.

However, many U.S. managers may not be as good at dealing with ambiguity as we would like to think. Situations in which the outcomes are highly unpredictable can create intolerable anxiety. Each culture teaches people a preferred strategy for responding to unstructured and confusing situations. Thus, in the U.S., continual data-gathering combined with procedures for constantly cross-examining decisions helps managers cope with uncertainty.

At the Stable Pole

In societies near the Stable pole, people are more likely to shun unpredictable situations. They become nervous when encountering change, conflict, or competition in their work and try to avoid them through clearly defined rules, regulations, and policies. By eschewing unclear situations and unfamiliar risks, they hope to avoid the stress of mistakes and failure.

Continuity is valued and change is considered disruptive. For example, in Japan, when new management is brought in, there is an emphasis on preserving earlier rituals and traditions rather than supplanting them.

In the Workplace

These values affect the following preferences.

Structure of work life. Presently in the U.S., companies are experimenting with flattened hierarchical structures, decentralization, matrix management, cross-functional teams, and other ways of restructuring organizations and the flow of work.

In cultures where stability is valued more than dynamism, employees may become confused when their work situation is too fluid and not well-defined. Detailed job descriptions are preferred. Subordinates want their managers to have precise answers to most of the questions they raise about their work. A structure in which a subordinate can have two bosses is seen as absurd. Workers strongly feel a need for rules and procedures.

Paradoxically, these rules and procedures then may be ignored by individuals, as for example when a manager seeks "forgiveness rather than permission" for a special project initiative.

"One best way" answers to problems. Believing in their own ability to respond dynamically to novel situations, U.S. managers tend to presume that a "new" right answer can be found to address most management issues. As indicated by the popularity of research on best practices, U.S. management often believes that there is one best way of structuring an organization, supervising employees, designing a compensation system, and so on. The assumption is that empirical inquiry or trial and error can be used to devise solutions to most problems. Changing management fads are also an example of this: Each fad is perceived for a time as a solution to all that ails management.

In dealing with the complexity of running large domestic or multinational companies, strong staff groups often impose these generic standards or operating rules on diverse parts of their organizations. As is evident in the global arena, one-best-way applications are often incompatible with local needs. For this reason, the efforts of U.S. companies to export the U.S. version of procedures or of products and advertising can sometimes fail.

Different people and ideas. The U.S. Constitution guarantees its citizens the right to hold dissenting views. A diversity of beliefs is tolerated. All people are relatively free to express viewpoints that may seem deviant to others and to challenge the authority of existing institutions. Petitions, demonstrations, and boycotts are acceptable because there is a commitment to upholding the values that create a pluralistic society.

These principles have found their way into the workplace as well; managers strive, not always successfully, to implement affirmative-action policies and other practices that support diversity.

In several parts of the world this tolerance in the U.S. of people with different ideas is viewed with suspicion and regarded as morally backward. Both socially and politically, the practice in these parts of the world is to repress and even persecute subpopulations whose origins can be traced to another ethnic, racial, or religious background—their views seem inferior to those held by the ruling majority. This makes intergroup strife more likely, and such tensions find their way into the workplace as well.

Thus, for example, in order to run an efficient manufacturing operation abroad, a U.S. manager may find that the company's human resources department has to adopt a policy of hiring people who come from the same ethnic or linguistic or tribal background. Otherwise, interactions that provoke work disruption and even violence are likely.

Means of Knowledge Acquisition: Active-Reflective

Which is valued more as a means of acquiring information and knowledge—action or reflection?

At the Active Pole

In societies near the Active pole, people value empirical data, facts, and practical experience. They are willing to experiment and solve problems by trial and error. Case studies, experiential learning, and fieldwork appeal to them. Overall, an experimental and data-based approach to identifying and solving problems feels natural to them.

People in the U.S. learn very early in life that effective people are active. Action is almost always preferred over inaction, and people routinely fill their days and weeks with activities.

Respect for manual and physical labor is also an expression of the value placed on doing, not thinking. Unlike many other parts of the world, even socioeconomically well-placed individuals attend to their own household tasks and errands, such as yard work, exterior and interior painting, cooking, and other chores. There seems to be such an aversion to "just sitting around and doing nothing" that even vacations are planned to be activity-oriented and busy.

At the Reflective Pole

In societies near the Reflective pole, people value conceptual models and general principles as guides for action. They prefer to think things through or develop an intuitive feel for a problem before attempting a solution. They admire intellectual brilliance and deductive reasoning. Overall, they favor great thinkers over doers and respect theoretical and intuitive approaches to solving problems.

In France and Germany, for example, people seem to feel a greater need to be reflective, avoid the possibility of impetuous action, and refrain from quick answers to questions or issues. They tend to approach problems more deliberately, seeking first to decide on an overall conceptual scheme and build a situational theory and then to proceed to problem solving.

Managers in several other countries, especially those of the Far East, use the passage of time to create a reflective perspective; delaying and waiting gives time a chance to disclose more of the relevant factors affecting a situation and allows those involved to become less emotional. In the U.S., executives tend to believe they must respond to problematic situations quickly.

As another example, in China it is important to be a patient listener, and young people are expected to learn this. The Chinese do not hurry their conversations along as people from the U.S. do. It is not uncommon for long pauses to occur and for people to be quiet and wait for their turn (Leong, 1994).

In the Workplace

These values lead to the following preferences.

Axiomatic versus pragmatic thinking. Asians with a Confucian heritage are much more likely to believe that all knowledge is a part of some universal natural order. In coping with a specific problem or issue, they seek to discover universal principles, not the factors governing a specific situation. The views and experiences of someone in the situation may be of far less importance than the wisdom of sages, who may have no interest in or experience with the practical world. In fact, there is an emphasis on ignoring individual views and experiences.

In contrast, people in the U.S. take great pride in being pragmatic. They are suspicious of too much theory, too many concepts, and certainly of ideas that have not been tested in the real world. They strongly believe that each individual has to learn what is important at a specific time in order to apply it to a specific situation. They presume that the learner, particularly if he or she is an adult, can contribute a good deal to problem solving.

Analytic approach to solving problems. U.S. managers also like to approach problems analytically. They assume that most of the problems they confront have straightforward cause-and-effect relationships. They are inclined to deal with problems in a highly linear way. For example, poor employee performance is seen as being caused by a lack of motivation or incentives; selling a new cereal is understood as depending on finding the right symbols for a specific market niche.

There is also a value placed on using the correct method for deriving answers to problems, and the preferred method is that of science. Managers like to rely on presumably objective, quantitative methods to find answers— for instance, by using market research, employee surveys, or operations research. Faith is placed in systematic, impersonal, and scientific inquiry to discover how many people are likely to buy a new gadget, how a product should be designed, or how to resolve other business issues.

In many other cultures, feelings and beliefs may be considered just as important in decision making as objective facts; intuitive, and even subjective, approaches may be preferred.

In most Asian countries, managers think in systems terms almost instinctively, in contrast to using a Western, compartmentalized and functional approach. Japanese companies are known for not publishing job descriptions, which build a box around the manager's responsibilities. Rather than always breaking problems and responsibilities into smaller and smaller discrete units, the Eastern view stresses looking for larger wholes and harmonious interrelationships.

As is becoming apparent to U.S. business leaders, the emphasis on rational and analytic modes of problem solving leads to a kind of compartmentalization that can cause managers to lose sight of processes and systems. The complexities of operating in today's business world can make insight, intuition, and even artistic and creative capabilities more useful than rationalistic, analytical skills. For example, instead of conceiving of human, technical, environmental, and political issues as distinct or in conflict, policy-makers may need to find answers that preserve or enhance harmony in the total system.

Strategic and long-term decisions. In general, managers in most cultures tend to focus on short-term operational issues. Priority is given to putting out fires rather than clarifying long-term goals. The balance between short- and long-term focus, however, varies from culture to culture and may be related to preferences for doing versus thinking.

A comparison of the behaviors of U.S. managers and their European counterparts who participated in a six-hour business simulation showed that U.S. managers tended, on an average, to make twenty-five percent more decisions. The Europeans preferred to gather data and then to engage in long discussions about that data. They seemed to enjoy the intellectual exercise of problem solving, often prolonging the discussions. Though fewer decisions were made, the decisions that were made, in general, addressed the long-term well-being of the organization (Wall & McHenry, 1989).

Perspective on Time: Scarce-Plentiful

Is the orientation to the use of time urgent or relaxed?

At the Scarce Pole

People from societies near the Scarce pole treat time as a limited resource that must be used efficiently. They prefer to spend time purposefully and with intensity. There is a sense that every minute counts. They also prefer to go about their tasks sequentially, working toward the future from the present.

Managers in the U.S. are inculcated with the strong value that time is money and must be used as efficiently as any other resource. Managers continuously bemoan wasted time: "I don't have anything to show what I accomplished today"; "Time just flew by and I never got to do any real work." Meetings, particularly, take a great deal of abuse, because getting together to socialize, exchange information, and resolve issues is not considered real work.

In the U.S., a whole industry has grown up around time-management systems and formal training programs on using time effectively. Thus, people cultivate the illusion that they are controlling time when, in fact, time seems to be controlling them.

At the Plentiful Pole

People from societies near the Plentiful pole think of time as infinitely available. Timelines and deadlines are seen as an expression of intent, not commitment. There is always a tomorrow. They prefer a life that evolves from the moment and allows for multiple and simultaneous involvements with the people and opportunities around them.

In cultures where agrarian traditions have continued until recently, time is dealt with quite differently and is not perceived as scarce. "When God made time you must remember he made a lot of it" is an old Scottish saying, and "Time is an endless river" to some. Therefore, time can be "wasted" without guilt.

In the Workplace

These values affect the following preferences.

The precise use of time. A concomitant of modern industrialization is a unique view of time and a special way of using it. Getting work done in organizations in a way that meets the needs of internal technology and external markets requires coordination. The essence of coordination is regulating time and interlocking various activities by the clock-beat of schedules. Time is thus the primary mechanism by which organizations become organized.

For U.S. managers, appointment times and schedules are often sacrosanct. Efficiency requires precision. Thus, there is an abruptness and choppiness about interaction, a compulsion to quickly get to the business at hand, to have one's life ruled by the clock. Keeping to the schedule, even though it may be self-imposed, is considered very important. The pace of a manager's life is set by the clock and the schedule almost as much as the pace of an assembly-line worker's life.

In countries where time is elastic, specific appointment times are often more wish than reality. Looseness about schedules can be observed in the countries of southern Europe. This can reach extremes, of course, as in Latin America, where one frequently hears, "If not today, then tomorrow or the next day. No hurry."

The linear use of time. U.S. managers also have been taught to be very linear and to sequence interactions—one thing at a time. It is considered impolite to take a call from A while talking with B or to speak with both at once on different subjects or to be observing the factory floor while talking to a supervisor.

In other cultures it is not unusual to see a manager engaged in several diverse activities at the same time. Managers may hold several small meetings simultaneously—talking to one person on the phone and to another who is standing in the office doorway. These managers see no need to string out these interactions in separate segments. Further, the sequence of what gets done is also in flux.

It is likely that the profound coordination requirements of modern technologies and fast-paced organizational events require the ability to cope simultaneously with a number of people and issues. The one-thing-at-a-time approach may not only be too slow but also do an injustice to the true complexity of the problems of running an organization.

Past, present, and future. In many Southeast Asian countries, as well as China and Japan, great value is placed on the past and on the continuities of life. Symbols that represent the past are very much in use. Ancestors are revered, as are senior members of the organization or the family. At the same time these countries may be very forward-looking technically and commercially.

In the mobile U.S. society, people are always leaving their roots behind, literally and figuratively. Life in organizations in the U.S. is very much oriented to the present and future. Many U.S. managers are anxious to remove reminders of the work of previous leaders. There is little respect for the antecedents of their own rule and not much more respect for the past or tradition.

Experienced U.S. managers who have worked in Japan are impressed with how change is handled there. In the U.S. there is a tendency to start from scratch by throwing out the old and installing the new. The Japanese are more likely to perceive the new as building on the old, not replacing it.

Outlook on Life: Doing-Being

Is mastery over nature or harmony with nature preferred? Is life experienced as an outcome of human effort or the workings of destiny or divine will?

At the Doing Pole

In societies near the Doing pole, people want to actively shape their lives and surroundings. They value planful activities that improve their situations. Technology is cherished as a means of making progress toward a better or more fulfilled life. Being in control of their lives and environment is seen as essential.

People from the U.S. believe that their destiny is controlled by their own actions, not fate. It feels natural to control nature, as is indicated for example by ongoing research on how weather conditions can be changed or how the gender of babies can be predetermined. Problems are seen as the result of poor planning or laziness, not bad luck. Moreover, many individuals try to influence their work and natural environment in order to protect and enhance their own self-interest.

Managers, too, believe that most problems, inside and outside the organization, can be solved by prepared, well-meaning people. Nature and human institutions are perceived as almost infinitely manipulable.

This outlook is reflected in the following proverbs, popular in the U.S.: "Where there's a will, there's a way"; "If at first you don't succeed, try, try again"; "The difficult we do at once; the impossible takes a little longer."

At the Being Pole

In societies near the Being pole, people feel a need to live in unity with, as well as within the given limits of, their natural surroundings. They see themselves as a part of their environment and accept what life gives them. They prefer a steady and relaxed way of life that allows them to live in the here and now. They trust that things will work out in the greater scheme of things.

Much more is perceived as immutable. Humans are seen as puny compared to the forces of nature and the world. People tend to accept things as they are. After all, how much can one really accomplish in the face of the forces arrayed against change?

One of the most frustrating experiences of a Peace Corps volunteer in India had to do with his effort to protect the crops of a number of farmers in the village to which he had been assigned. When he learned of an impending infestation that would likely destroy an entire crop, he ordered the appropriate insecticide, but the farmers refused to use it. For them, the success of the crop had already been determined by God, and it was unrealistic to consider human intervention (Sayles, research notes).

In the Workplace

In organizational life these values affect the following orientations.

Commitment to work and economic values. How important is work and material gain in the lives of employees? From the point of view of the U.S. manager, it is critically important to have employees who perceive work as a major source of self-identification and personal satisfaction. In many parts of the world, this is simply not true.

Some traditional societies don't even have a word for work; activities related to earning a living, maintaining social relations, religious observances, child-rearing, resting, and celebrating all blur together in the course of a day, season, and year. In many countries, it is common for managers to seek to convert some business activities into social events.

Distinguishing between *work* and *not-work* is not always simple. When a fisherman plays a song that is supposed to attract fish, should that be considered work? If a day is taken to have a local shaman come in and bless the machinery in a new factory before workers will consent to work there, is that a workday, part of the commencement of operations, or a lost workday?

Except for business lunches and entertaining out-of-town customers, many U.S. managers find it difficult to socialize at work or during off-hours for the sake of building relationships. The future benefits appear amorphous, and losing time seems inefficient. They feel that one must keep busy constantly on activities which are unambiguously work. Conversely, when they relax, with family or friends, work should have no part.

Thus, it is not surprising that U.S. managers find it strange that managers elsewhere devote long evenings to mixing work-related discussions with drinking and singing. On the other hand, because they see business relationships as simply another way for people to join with each other and achieve mutually valued objectives, non-U.S. managers find it strange and intimidating that their U.S. counterparts spend so much time and money involving lawyers in business agreements.

Optimism about the future. The very concept of progress—that human welfare tends to improve over time and that activity can be linked to results—is a relatively recent western European invention. The belief that there is a relationship between personal effort (specifically hard work) and results is culture-based.

In part, attitudes toward work are dependent on historical factors that shape how employees see the future. Cultures that are periodically racked by civil wars, expropriation, and social mayhem, where the future looks bleak and tomorrow is likely to be worse than today, discourage hard work, initiative, and planning ahead.

In order to feel that they can be effective in organizations, managers and workers must have some confidence about the future. Only in cultures with growing economies, mobility, and status by achievement do people sense that they can get out of life what they "deserve" or what they "put into it." Where optimism about the future is lacking, it is unlikely that there will be sustained energy devoted to work-oriented activity, particularly if it involves any element of sacrificing short-term returns for longer-term benefits.

One of the underlying issues in having confidence about the future is the stability of the system. The U.S. system has been one of the most stable in the world during the past century. Therefore, stability is an implicit part of the managerial and organizational models created by academics and taught to upcoming business managers. Assuming the stability of the system is not appropriate for many other parts of the world and may not be appropriate for the U.S. in the twenty-first century.

Traditional religions and the world of work. U.S. managers can feel frustrated in a world where fate determines events and where the only source of optimism is the hope that the next life may be a better one.

Many variants on the pessimistic-fatalistic theme are religious in origin. The term *Islam* stems from the Arabic verb meaning "to submit." Muslims believe that the will of Allah intercedes in the most minute of human events and is unpredictable and often inexplicable. Thus a manager may be greeted by a fatalistic shrug when asking about some construction work that is progressing poorly.

Just as people in many countries do not compartmentalize work and family, they also may not compartmentalize religion, placing it above all other institutions except, perhaps, family. These types of cultural orientations toward religion are unfamiliar to people in the U.S., and to them it seems inappropriate to place religion in so powerful a role.

A recent BBC report described a Buddhist ceremony in Japan attended by senior executives of many prominent Japanese companies. The purpose was to propitiate the spirits of the electronic products and components that they were no longer producing. A more common practice is for a religious figure to visit a manufacturing plant to bless a new piece of equipment.

One U.S. executive assigned to a deeply religious country was able to broaden the scope of his understanding in this area. Initiating an alms box for the local Catholic church was, in his case, an excellent strategy to gain local respect. In that Catholic country, showing deference to local religious leaders was consistent with sound business practice. It was culturally congruent for the priest to visit the office to express appreciation and collect the offerings.

The idea that business has obligations to redistribute some of its wealth to religious institutions and that religious leaders have a role to play in business seems strange, if not inappropriate, to many managers from the U.S. and northern Europe. The religious obligations of the business sector in many societies can be disconcerting for executives not used to such practices.

Using the Framework

Cultures evolve and are heterogeneous, interactive, and dynamic. The world is being reshaped by a large number of major events and trends that have occurred over the last ten to fifteen years such as the opening of former socialist economies; widespread privatization in many countries; the political disintegration of some nation-states; the relative decline of the economic hegemony of the U.S.; the development of new communication technologies; forced and voluntary migration; the changing role of women; accelerating attention to environmental concerns; and an increase in terrorism, violence, and crime (Behrman, 1995). Given this state of flux, it would be a mistake to think that your objective as a manager should be to use this learning framework to construct a neat model of a cultural group.

Nevertheless, using the framework can help you become aware of the dynamics of cross-cultural interactions, thus aiding you in managing them in the workplace. The four-step procedure described below will help you apply this framework.

1. Use the seven dimensions to observe your own and others' preferences in three domains of human behavior: relating to others, accomplishing work, and responding to change.
2. Construct a provisional hypothesis, or stereotype, by drawing on various sources of information, projecting how people from a particular culture are likely to behave.
3. Test and modify the hypothesis continually, based on your experiences.
4. Challenge yourself to grow personally by recognizing that your effectiveness as a manager depends on your ability to genuinely appreciate values that seem opposite to your own.

Use the Seven Dimensions

The first three dimensions encompass dilemmas that emerge when relating to others. These dilemmas, which represent opposing value orientations, are observed in the following behaviors:

1. *Source of Identity.* Do individuals define themselves by separating from or integrating with a group? Which of their group affiliations are most important to them—their religion? country? profession? employing organization?

2. *Goals and Means of Achievement.* Do the actions of individuals focus on achievements or relationships?

3. *Orientation to Authority.* How do individuals behave toward people who have greater or lesser status than their own?

The next three dimensions encompass dilemmas that surface when accomplishing work. The following behaviors are indicators:

4. *Response to Ambiguity.* Do individuals take on undefined tasks and use experimental methods or do they seek out defined tasks and use traditional methods?

5. *Means of Knowledge Acquisition.* Are individuals more likely to reflect or to act?

6. *Perspective on Time.* Is their use of time urgent or relaxed?

The final dimension encompasses dilemmas that emerge when responding to change or progress.

7. *Outlook on Life.* Do individuals seek control over events or do they favor accommodating themselves to events? Do their activities have a primarily economic or human focus?

By using these questions to query yourself and observe others, you can train yourself to detect how value preferences vary. Table 2 is a useful guide to behaviors and other indicators that can help you do this.

Construct a Provisional Hypothesis

The clues you uncover using the framework will assist you in predicting the behavior of cultural groups as well as individuals. It will guide you as you: (a) make observations of other cultures and individuals; (b) inquire into the behavior differences that are experienced when interacting with people different from you; (c) reflect on your own preferences and values; and (d) take actions that are situationally appropriate and stimulate further learning. As you apply this framework to various situations, you will gather information in a variety of ways that will enable you to construct as accurate a picture as possible of differing value orientations.

Test and Modify the Hypothesis Continually

Managers who are comfortable and communicate effectively with people of any culture seem to think about their relationships with people differently than most managers; they are willing to get to know and enjoy people who are not the same as they are (Hoopes, 1979; Ratiu, 1983).

For such managers, a general profile (for instance, the provisional hypothesis or stereotype that is constructed by using the framework) is continually tested and modified. The general profile is simply a "first best guess" (Adler, 1991, p. 72).

One-on-one interactions are then used to construct a more accurate description of the other person. These descriptions are not an explanation of the culturally different person from your own point of view but rather a sight line into his or her behavior from his or her point of view. After all, in most situations, adults in general seek to act effectively and present themselves in the best possible light. Over time, multiple cumulative interactions lead to cultural insight.

Challenge Yourself to Grow Personally

The person-to-person relationship is primary. The exchange between you and the other person is designed not to control the behavior of the other person but to understand it. The challenge is *not* to come to a quick conceptual conclusion about the other but to use your sense of the situation to intuitively guide the interaction and reach a tentative understanding of the other person that remains open to continual revision. The pragmatic need to work with people different from yourself governs the situation and personal evaluation is avoided.

In encountering another person in this way, you may need to review and modify your own opinions and attitudes, even letting go of some of your own values and beliefs. Because of the primacy of the in-the-moment one-on-one

Table 2
Applying the Learning Framework

DIMENSION	BEHAVIORS TO OBSERVE	OTHER INDICATORS Relating to Others
Source of Identity		
Individual	Separates from group?	Individuals are accountable. Career progress is valued. Private offices are common.
Collective	Integrates with group?	Loyalty to company is important. Loyalty to family or clan is typical.
Goals and Means of Achievement		
Tough	Focuses on achievements?	Competitive attitudes are prevalent. Work life is given priority.
Tender	Focuses on relationships?	Modesty is valued. Candor and directness are avoided.
Orientation to Authority		
Equal	Ignores differences in power, status, and authority?	Promotion is based on achievement record, not seniority, age, and so on
Unequal	Acknowledges differences in power, status, and authority?	Deference toward superiors is common. Authority is seldom delegated.

		Accomplishing Work
Response to Ambiguity		
Dynamic	Takes on undefined tasks using experimental methods?	Cross-functional teams are likely. Different people and ideas are valued.
Stable	Follows defined tasks using traditional methods?	Detailed job descriptions are used. "One best way" answers are preferred.
Means of Knowledge Acquisition		
Active	Acts first?	Practical approaches prevail. Short term is emphasized. Analytic and data-based approaches are valued.
Reflective	Reflects first?	Conceptual approaches prevail. Long term is emphasized. Intuition is valued.

		Responding to Change
Perspectives on Time		
Scarce	Uses time with urgency?	Meeting times are precise. Focus is on the future.
Plentiful	Uses time in a relaxed way?	Work/nonwork activities are undertaken at the same time. Present is seen as building on the past.
Outlook on Life		
Doing	Seeks to control events and has an economic focus?	Optimistic about the future. Work is an obligation to create a better future.
Being	Accommodates to events and has a human focus?	Higher powers such as destiny are seen as controlling future. Nonmaterial aspects of life are valued.

relationship, in the process of thinking through issues together, both of you may be changed.

An experienced senior executive from a multinational organization summarized this approach:

> You have to hear with your body besides paying attention with your ears and eyes when you listen to others. You discover what's of value to them. In order to persuade others, you have to uncover their worldview and framework.

What is important to remember is that by learning to think and act in ways that may be initially uncomfortable, managers do not have to give up their own ways of thinking and acting. By learning how to think and act in more than one way, they simply become versatile (Kaplan, 1996).

Conclusion

In this report we have sought to describe the major cultural issues that confront managers from the U.S. and elsewhere who work with diverse populations. Many of these issues call into question the comfortable but very culture-bound presumption that there is a right way and a wrong way to do business and to manage. Our discussion should assist you in surfacing some of your tacit assumptions about what organizations should be like, how employees should behave, and how decisions and work should be carried out.

There is often a bias, particularly in the U.S., that people are all basically alike and that the process of getting to know someone from another culture is not really very challenging. We hope this paper demonstrates beyond a doubt that, although we are all human, the worldviews of people from different cultures are not the same and that, although we may interact easily with a variety of people in social situations, working together effectively in business situations requires real cultural and personal insight. We also hope that we have illustrated how important it is to first become aware of your own value preferences so that the value preferences of others can be observed. These are initial steps.

The subsequent steps require you to ask yourself some difficult questions: Can you learn to observe how these value preferences play out when people from different cultures work with each other? Do you have the patience and persistence to draw out the invisible mental map that guides visible action? Can you surface the unconscious patterns of perceiving and thinking that condition the sentiments and behaviors that individuals express?

We believe that by learning to see situations from multiple points of view, you will be able to help your employees connect more effectively with each other. The social context of work has become very complex as a result of various factors: for instance, the free movement of labor and capital across borders, the decreasing costs of transport and telecommunication as a consequence of technological progress, and the open pursuit of prosperity and a higher standard of living among the developing nations of the world. Your capacity to create the conditions under which a diverse group of individuals can succeed is quickly becoming a crucial managerial skill.

Additional questions that you should consider include: Having observed the range of differences possible, can you tolerate those moments and situations in which diverse desires contend with each other for right of way? What are the behavioral adaptations required for people to work together? Finding the integrative solution to a problem is not always easy, but it is central to the task of collaborating across cultures. The interaction between people, as well as the interaction between people and problems, invariably creates friction and requires mutual adjustment.

How can you as a manager in today's world capitalize on friction? This is the final question we choose to raise. Mary Parker Follett (Graham, 1995, p. 68), a pioneering thinker who highlighted these issues in the context of an approach she called "integrative business management," phrased it well:

> All polishing is done by friction. The music of the violin we get by friction. We left the savage style when we discovered fire by friction. So we talk of the friction of mind on mind as a good thing.

References

Adler, N. J. (1991). *International dimensions of organizational behavior* (2nd ed.). Boston: PWS-KENT.

Behrman, J. N. (1995). *Cross-cultural impacts on international competitiveness.* (Available from Kenan-Flagler Business School, University of North Carolina at Chapel Hill, NC).

Bluedorn, A. C. (1995, August). New perspectives on assessing and using the organization culture construct in organization science. *Time: Exploring culture's temporal core.* Symposium conducted at the Academy of Management, Vancouver, British Columbia, Canada.

Bond, M. (1987). Chinese values and the search for culture-free dimensions of culture. *Journal of Cross-Cultural Psychology, 18*(2), 143-164.

Edwards, J. (1992). *Transit of Venus.* New York: Pantheon.

Graham, P. (Ed.). (1995). *Mary Parker Follett—Prophet of management: A celebration of writings from the 1920s.* Boston, MA: Harvard Business School Press.

Hall, E. T. (1981). *Beyond culture.* New York: Doubleday.

Hampden-Turner, C., & Trompenaars, A. (1993). *The seven cultures of capitalism: Value systems for creating wealth in the United States, Japan, Germany, France, Britain, Sweden, and the Netherlands* (1st ed.). New York: Currency.

Hofstede, G. (1980). *Culture's consequences: International differences in work-related values.* Beverly Hills, CA: Sage.

Hofstede, G. (1991). *Culture and organizations: Software of the mind.* London: McGraw-Hill.

Hofstede, G., & Bond, M. H. (1988, Spring). The Confucius connection: From cultural roots to economic growth. *Organizational Dynamics, 16*(4), 4-21.

Hoopes, D. S. (1979). Intercultural communication concepts and psychology of intercultural experiences. In M. D. Pusch (Ed.), *Multicultural education: A cross-cultural training approach.* Yarmouth, ME: Intercultural Press.

Hoppe, M. H. (1990). *A comparative study of country elites: International differences in work-related values and learning and their implications for management training and development.* Unpublished doctoral dissertation, The University of North Carolina at Chapel Hill.

House, R. J., Hanges, P., Agar, M., & Quintanilla, A. R. (1995). *Globe: The global leadership and organizational behavior effectiveness research program.* Philadelphia: The Wharton School, Department of Management, The University of Pennsylvania.

Kaplan, R. E. (1996). *Forceful leadership and enabling leadership: You can do both.* Greensboro, NC: Center for Creative leadership.

Kluckhohn, F. R., & Strodtbeck, F. L. (1961). *Variations in value orientations.* Westport, CT: Greenwood Press.

Kohls, L. R. (1981). *Developing intercultural awareness* (1st ed.). Washington, DC: SIETAR International.

Kroeber, A. L., & Kluckhohn, C. (1952). *Culture: Critical review of concepts and definitions* (Vol. 1, No. 1). Cambridge, MA: Peabody Museum.

Laurent, A. (1983). The cultural diversity of Western conceptions of management. *International Studies of Management and Organization, 13*(1-2), 75-96.

Leong, F. T. L. (1994). *Guidelines for doing business with the Chinese.* Unpublished manuscript, Ohio State University.

Mrydal, G. (1968). *Asian drama: An inquiry into the poverty of nations.* New York: Pantheon.

Noer, D. M. (1993). *Healing the wounds: Overcoming the trauma of layoffs and revitalizing downsized organizations.* San Francisco: Jossey-Bass.

Ratiu, I. (1983). Thinking internationally: A comparison of how international executives learn. *International Studies of Management and Organization, 13*(1-2), 139-150.

Rokeach, M. (1973). *The nature of human values.* New York: Basic Books.

Ronen, S. (1986). *Comparative and multinational management.* New York: Wiley.

Sayles, L. R. (1995). *Leadership for turbulent times.* Greensboro, NC: Center for Creative Leadership.

Schein, E. H. (1985). *Organizational culture and leadership.* San Francisco: Jossey-Bass.

Schwartz, S. H. (1993). *Beyond individualism-collectivism: New cultural dimensions of values.* Unpublished paper, The Hebrew University of Jerusalem.

Scott-Stevens, S. (1991, November). *Value orientations and technology transfer.* Paper presented at the Pragmatics of Intercultural Project Management program, American Anthropological Association Annual Meeting, Chicago.

Triandis, H. C. (1995). *Individualism and collectivism.* Boulder, CO: Westview.

Triandis, H. C., McCusker, C., & Hui, C. H. (1990). Multimethod probes of individualism and collectivism. *Journal of Personality and Social Psychology, 59*(5), 1006-1020.

Trompenaars, F. (1993). *Riding the waves of culture: Understanding cultural diversity in business.* London: The Economist Books.

Wall, S. J., & McHenry, R. (1989). North Americans, Europeans, and 1992. *Issues & Observations, 9*(4), 1-3.

Appendix:
Models of Cultural Difference

Currently, several authors have developed models of cultural differences; the framework described in this report is based on an integration of existing literature (Bluedorn, 1995; Bond, 1987; Hampden-Turner & Trompenaars, 1993; Hofstede, 1980, 1991; Hofstede & Bond, 1988; House, Hanges, Agar, & Quintanilla, 1995; Kluckhohn & Strodtbeck, 1961; Triandis, 1995; Trompenaars, 1993). Our focus, however, is not on developing a theory of cultural differences but on developing a conceptual tool that can be used by executives, managers, and employees.

Therefore, we have included a table (Table A1) that shows the equivalence between models by highlighting conceptual similarities independent of terms and labels. The correspondence between concepts across models is not always precise; but the table can help interested readers to explore related concepts by referring to original sources.

Obviously, social scientists are observing the same behaviors; but as they try to map out the differences between these behaviors by developing models, they discover that cultures seem to use an interconnected set of values to guide their members about how they should perceive, interpret, and react to their lives. So cultures are value systems that maintain themselves by shaping the behavior of the individuals within them.

What is not clear is how these values are interconnected. In other words, an observed behavior may be caused not by one value, but by a combination of values. So, for example, is an activity orientation related to perceptions of time? Is the use of intuition related to a human focus? How is universalism related to individualism? These relationships are presently not apparent and account for the differences between models.

The table therefore illustrates how far researchers have traveled in their effort to map out and name a territory that is invisible and largely unexplored. "Territory," in this case, is the same as "collective mind of cultural groups" (if one assumes that a group does in fact have a collective mind). This invisible territory is made visible as behavior differences.

In this context we hope the table serves the reader by simplifying—but not being simplistic about—the current understanding of the complexity of cultural differences.

Table A1
Conceptual Similarities between the Learning Framework and
Other Models of Cultural Difference

Learning Framework (1996)	Hofstede (1980, 1991)	Kluckhohn & Strodtbeck (1961)	Hofstede & Bond (1988)
• Individual-Collective	• Individualism-Collectivism	• Relational orientation (collective, individual) • Space orientation (public, private, mixed)	• Collectivism –integration –moral discipline
• Tough-Tender			• Human-heartedness –kindness –patience –courtesy
• Equal-Unequal	• Power distance	• Relational orientation (hierarchical)	
• Dynamic-Stable	• Uncertainty-Avoidance	• Human nature • Relationship to nature	
• Active-Reflective –pace –intuition –pragmatism			
• Scarce-Plentiful –punctuality –polychronicity –time horizon		• Time orientation (past, present, future)	• Confucian dynamism
• Doing-Being –control –human focus	• Masculine-Feminine	• Activity orientation (being, doing, controlling)	

Note. Bulleted items are dimensions of difference; subentries preceded by hyphens are components of the dimensions.

Table A1
Conceptual Similarities between the Learning Framework and
Other Models of Cultural Difference (continued)

Trompenaars (1993)	Hampden-Turner & Trompenaars (1993)	Triandis (1986)	Bluedorn (1995)	House, Hanges, Agar, & Quintanilla (1995)
• Individualist-Collectivist • Universalist-Particularist • Specific-Diffuse	• Individualism-Communitarianism • Universalism-Particularism	• Individualism-Collectivism –family integrity –interdependence with sociability –separation from in-groups –self-reliance/ with hedonism		• Individualism-Collectivism
				• Humanistic-Impersonal
• Achievement-Ascription oriented	• Achieved-Ascribed • Equality-Hierarchy			• Power Stratification-Egalitarianism
• Neutral-Affective				• Tolerance-Intolerance of uncertainty
	• Analyzing-Integrating • Inner directed-Outer directed		• Time –pace	
• Future-Present-Past oriented	• Sequence-Synchronization		–punctuality –polychronicity –time horizon	• Future-Present
• Internal-External oriented				• Masculinity-Femininity • Achievement orientation

CENTER FOR CREATIVE LEADERSHIP PUBLICATIONS LIST

NEW RELEASES

IDEAS INTO ACTION GUIDEBOOKS

Ongoing Feedback: How to Get It, How to Use It Kirkland & Manoogian (1998, Stock #400) $8.95*

Reaching Your Development Goals McCauley & Martineau (1998, Stock #401) $8.95*

Becoming a More Versatile Learner Dalton (1998, Stock #402) $8.95

Giving Feedback to Subordinates Buron & McDonald-Mann (1999, Stock #403) $8.95*

Three Keys to Development: Defining and Meeting Your Leadership Challenges Browning & Van Velsor (1999, Stock #404) $8.95*

Feedback That Works: How to Build and Deliver Your Message Weitzel (2000, Stock #405) $8.95*

Communicating Across Cultures Prince & Hoppe (2000, Stock #406) $8.95

Learning From Life: Turning Life's Lessons into Leadership Experience Ruderman & Ohlott (2000, Stock #407) $8.95

Keeping Your Career on Track: Twenty Success Strategies Chappelow & Leslie (2001, Stock #408) $8.95

Preparing for Development: Making the Most of Formal Leadership Programs Martineau & Johnson (2001, Stock #409) $8.95*

Choosing an Executive Coach Kirkland & Hart (2001, Stock #410) $8.95

Setting Your Development Goals: Start with Your Values Sternbergh & Weitzel (2001, Stock #411) $8.95*

Do You Really Need a Team? Kossler & Kanaga (2001, Stock #412) $8.95

Building Resiliency: How to Thrive in Times of Change Pulley & Wakefield (2001, Stock #413) $8.95

How to Form a Team: Five Keys to High Performance Kanaga & Kossler (2001, Stock #414) $8.95

Using Your Executive Coach Hart & Kirkland (2001, Stock #415) $8.95

Managing Conflict with Your Boss Sharpe & Johnson (2002, Stock #416) $8.95

How to Launch a Team: Start Right for Success Kanaga & Prestridge (2002, Stock #417) $8.95

The Deep Blue Sea: Rethinking the Source of Leadership Drath (2001, Stock #2068) $27.95

Discovering the Leader in You Lee & King (2001, Stock #2067) $32.95

Emerging Leaders: An Annotated Bibliography Deal, Peterson, & Gaylor-Loflin (2001, Stock #352) $20.00

Executive Coaching: An Annotated Bibliography Douglas & Morley (2000, Stock #347) $20.00*

Executive Selection: Strategies for Success Sessa & Taylor (2000, Stock #2057) $34.95*

The Human Side of Knowledge Management: An Annotated Bibliography Mayer (2000, Stock #349) $20.00

The Leader's Edge: Six Creative Competencies for Navigating Complex Challenges Palus & Horth (2002, Stock #2116) $29.95

Leadership Resources: A Guide to Training and Development Tools (8th ed.) Schwartz & Gimbel (2000, Stock #348) $49.95*

Managerial Effectiveness in a Global Context Leslie, Dalton, Ernst, & Deal (2002, Stock #184 .... $35.00

Standing at the Crossroads: Next Steps for High-Achieving Women Ruderman & Ohlott (2002, Stock #2117) $26.95

Success for the New Global Manager Dalton, Ernst, Deal, & Leslie (2002, Stock #2111) $29.95

BEST-SELLERS

Breaking Free: A Prescription for Personal and Organizational Change Noer (1997, Stock #271) $36.95

Breaking the Glass Ceiling: Can Women Reach the Top of America's Largest Corporations? (Updated Edition) Morrison, White, & Van Velsor (1992, Stock #236A) $13.00

The Center for Creative Leadership Handbook of Leadership Development McCauley, Moxley, & Van Velsor (Eds.) (1998, Stock #201) $75.00*

Choosing 360: A Guide to Evaluating Multi-rater Feedback Instruments for Management Development Van Velsor, Leslie, & Fleenor (1997, Stock #334) $15.00*

Choosing Executives: A Research Report on the Peak Selection Simulation Deal, Sessa, & Taylor (1999, Stock #183) $20.00*

Coaching for Action: A Report on Long-term Advising in a Program Context Guthrie (1999, Stock #181) $20.00*

The Complete Inklings: Columns on Leadership and Creativity Campbell (1999, Stock #343) $20.00

Eighty-eight Assignments for Development in Place Lombardo & Eichinger (1989, Stock #136) $15.00*

Enhancing 360-degree Feedback for Senior Executives: How to Maximize the Benefits and Minimize the Risks Kaplan & Palus (1994, Stock #160) $7.50*

Executive Selection: A Research Report on What Works and What Doesn't Sessa, Kaiser, Taylor, & Campbell (1998, Stock #179) $30.00*

Feedback to Managers (3rd Edition) Leslie & Fleenor (1998, Stock #178) $20.00*

Four Essential Ways that Coaching Can Help Executives Witherspoon & White (1997, Stock #175) $10.00

High Flyers: Developing the Next Generation of Leaders McCall (1997, Stock #293) $29.95

How to Design an Effective System for Developing Managers and Executives Dalton & Hollenbeck (1996, Stock #158) $15.00*

If I'm In Charge Here, Why Is Everybody Laughing? Campbell (1984, Stock #205) $9.95*

If You Don't Know Where You're Going You'll Probably End Up Somewhere Else Campbell (1974, Stock #203) $9.95*

Internalizing Strengths: An Overlooked Way of Overcoming Weaknesses in Managers Kaplan (1999, Stock #182) $15.00

International Success: Selecting, Developing, and Supporting Expatriate Managers Wilson & Dalton (1998, Stock #180) $15.00*

Leadership and Spirit Moxley (1999, Stock #2035) $36.00

The Lessons of Experience: How Successful Executives Develop on the Job McCall, Lombardo, & Morrison (1988, Stock #211) $28.00

Making Common Sense: Leadership as Meaning-making in a Community of Practice Drath & Palus (1994, Stock #156) $15.00

Maximizing the Value of 360-degree Feedback Tornow, London, & CCL Associates (1998, Stock #295) $45.00*

Perspectives on Dialogue: Making Talk Developmental for Individuals and Organizations Dixon (1996, Stock #168) $20.00

Positive Turbulence: Developing Climates for Creativity, Innovation, and Renewal Gryskiewicz (1999, Stock #2031) $35.00

Preventing Derailment: What To Do Before It's Too Late Lombardo & Eichinger (1989, Stock #138) ... $25.00

Should 360-degree Feedback Be Used Only for Developmental Purposes? Bracken, Dalton, Jako, McCauley, Pollman, with Preface by Hollenbeck (1997, Stock #335) $15.00*

Take the Road to Creativity and Get Off Your Dead End Campbell (1977, Stock #204) $9.95*

Twenty-two Ways to Develop Leadership in Staff Managers Eichinger & Lombardo (1990, Stock #144) $15.00

BIBLIOGRAPHIES

Geographically Dispersed Teams: An Annotated Bibliography Sessa, Hansen, Prestridge, & Kossler (1999, Stock #346) $20.00*

High-Performance Work Organizations: Definitions, Practices, and an Annotated Bibliography Kirkman, Lowe, & Young (1999, Stock #342) $20.00

Management Development through Job Experiences: An Annotated Bibliography McCauley & Brutus (1998, Stock #337) $10.00

Selection at the Top: An Annotated Bibliography Sessa & Campbell (1997, Stock #333) $20.00*

Succession Planning: An Annotated Bibliography Eastman (1995, Stock #324) $20.00*

Using 360-degree Feedback in Organizations: An Annotated Bibliography Fleenor & Prince (1997, Stock #338) $15.00*

Workforce Reductions: An Annotated Bibliography Hickok (1999, Stock #344) $20.00*

SPECIAL PACKAGES

Executive Selection Package (Stock #710C; includes 157, 164, 179, 180, 183, 333, 345, 2057) $100.00

Feedback Guidebook Package (Stock #724; includes 400, 403, 405) $17.95

Human Resource Professionals Information Package (Stock #717C; includes 136, 158, 179, 180, 182, 201, 324, 334, 348—includes complimentary copy of guidebook 409) $150.00

Individual Leadership Development Package (Stock #726; includes 401, 404, 409, 411) $26.95

Personal Growth, Taking Charge, and Enhancing Creativity (Stock #231; includes 203, 204, 205) $25.00

Select Sourcebook Package (Stock #727; includes 178, 324, 344, 346, 347, 348) $100.00

The 360 Collection (Stock #720C; includes 160, 178, 295, 334, 335, 338—includes complimentary copies of guidebooks contained in Feedback Guidebook Package above) $100.00

Discounts are available. Please write for a catalog. Address your request to: Publication, Center for Creative Leadership, P.O. Box 26300, Greensboro, NC 27438-6300, 336-545-2810, or fax to 336-282-3284. Purchase your publications from our online bookstore at **www.ccl.org/publications**. All prices subject to change.

*Indicates publication is also part of a package.

ORDER FORM

Or e-mail your order via the Center's online bookstore at www.ccl.org

Name _____ Title _____

Organization _____

Mailing Address _____
(street address required for mailing)

City/State/Zip _____

Telephone _____ FAX _____
(telephone number required for UPS mailing)

Quantity	Stock No.	Title	Unit Cost	Amount

CCL's Federal ID Number is 237-07-9591.

Subtotal	
Shipping and Handling (U.S. shipping rate $4 for 1st book, $0.95 for each additional book; International shipping rate $20 for 1st book, $5 for each additional book)	
NC residents add 6.5% sales tax; CA residents add 7.5% sales tax; CO residents add 6% sales tax	
TOTAL	

METHOD OF PAYMENT
(ALL orders for less than $100 must be PREPAID.)

❏ Check or money order enclosed (payable to Center for Creative Leadership).

❏ Purchase Order No. _____ (Must be accompanied by this form.)

❏ Charge my order, plus shipping, to my credit card:
　　❏ American Express　❏ Discover　❏ MasterCard　❏ Visa

ACCOUNT NUMBER:_____ EXPIRATION DATE: MO.____ YR.____

NAME AS APPEARS ON CARD: _____

SIGNATURE OF CARD HOLDER: _____

❏ Please put me on your mailing list.

Publication • Center for Creative Leadership • P.O. Box 26300
Greensboro, NC 27438-6300
336-545-2810 • FAX 336-282-3284

_____

_____

_____

CENTER FOR CREATIVE LEADERSHIP
PUBLICATION
P.O. Box 26300
Greensboro, NC 27438-6300